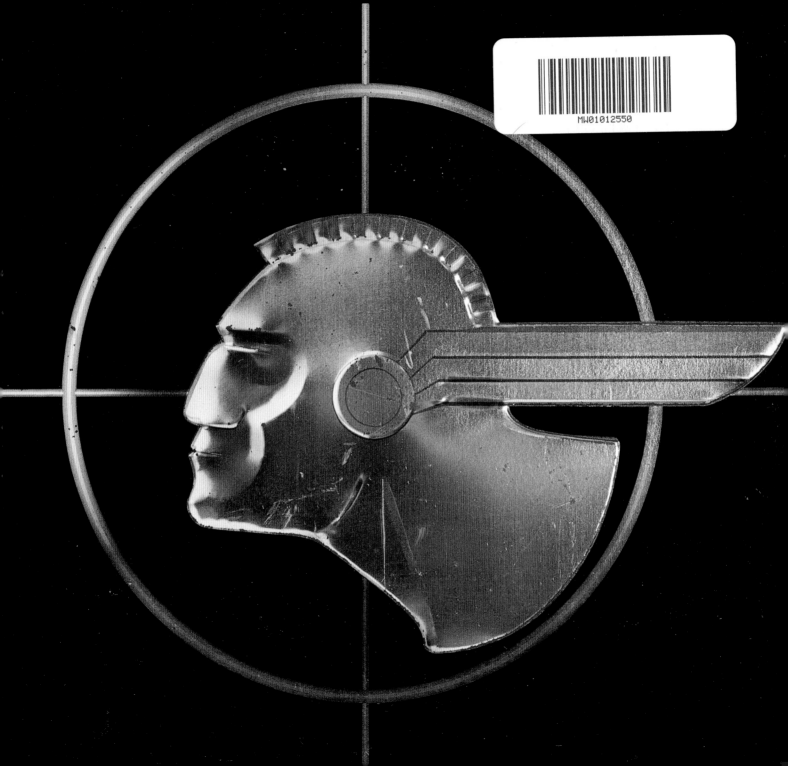

Brightwork

KEN STEACY

photographs by
Rob d'Estrubé

CHRONICLE BOOKS
SAN FRANCISCO

ACKNOWLEDGMENTS

Collecting artifacts of any kind, arranging them into a semblance of order, and then creating a book about them is both a solitary and a collaborative effort. I'd like to express my appreciation to the following people who made it happen:

Thanx to Scott Caple, who got the ball rolling by moving to Los Angeles and buying that vintage pile of Detroit iron, whose hood ornament first inspired me; and to "Junky Jack" Thornborrow, who gave me my first goddess (in more ways than one). May the road rise to meet you guys!

Special Thanx to José "Dirty Fingers" Armitage, Jim Colwill, and Bob Miller, my homeboys, who did so much to help build my collection (and shared theirs for inclusion in this book); Mayor Terry Jarvis who pushed me over the top (be sure to check out Vintage Auto Parts next time you're driving through Grace, WA); and author/collectors Robert Ames, Lynn Huntsburger, Dan Smith, and Bill Williams, whose books provided much inspiration (and in Lynn's case, more hood ornaments).

Special Deluxe Thanx to Ian "The Wanker" Rossiter, Frank Tosczak, and Dan Rippon, craftsmen extraordinaire, for restoration, baseage, and de-snurging.

Super Deluxe Thanx to my editor Alan Rapp, art director Pamela Geismar, and the rest of the gang at Chronicle Books—*non plus ultra*; to Rob d'Estrubé, for his superb photographic skills and remarkable patience; to Nick Porcino, Andrew Pratt and Liam Regan for prepress expertise; and to Doug Coupland for his perfect preface.

Super Deluxe Custom Thanx to my wonderful wife Joan Thornborrow-Steacy—you wouldn't be enjoying this tome were it not for her understanding (and tolerance) of my collecting disorder, folks!

Finally, just plain thanx to all the other collectors, swap meet vendors, and junkmen who, by off-loading these gems, provided the basis for my collection and this book.

All efforts have been made to trace the source and ownership of all copyrighted material in this book.

Additional Picture Credits: page 24, top: Walter Sanders/LIFE Magazine © Time Inc.; page 27, top: photograph © Gordon Coster; page 37, top: Courtesy Ford Motor Co.; page 41, top: © Universal Pictures; page 42, top: Courtesy Loewy Design; page 55, background: Courtesy Northrop Grumman; pages 68–69, 72–73, 94–95, backgrounds: Courtesy General Motors.

Library of Congress Cataloging-in-Publication Data available.

ISBN 0-8118-2663-5

Interior and cover design: Ken Steacy
Fonts: Stone Informal and Torpedo

Pages 1 and 120: 1950s Pontiac dealers' sign
Page 3: 1933–1936 Cadillac

Printed in Hong Kong

Distributed in Canada by
Raincoast Books
8680 Cambie Street
Vancouver, British Columbia
V6P 6M9

10 9 8 7 6 5 4 3 2 1

Chronicle Books
85 Second Street
San Francisco, CA 94105

www.chroniclebooks.com

CONTENTS

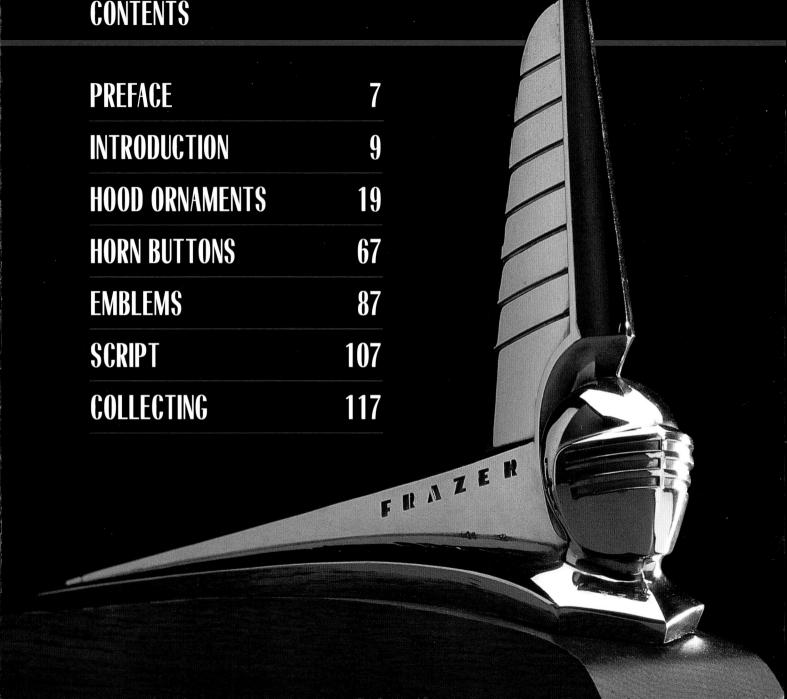

PREFACE

Should you ever be fortunate enough to visit Ken Steacy's basement, brace yourself: his collection of brightwork is huge, comprehensive, beautifully mounted, and smartly displayed. If you're a collector yourself (and who isn't?) Ken's brightwork museum—it really *must* be called a museum—will seriously make you reassess your dedication to whatever it is you collect.

Of course, collection without love is nothing more than neurotic gathering. And collecting without curation and maintenance is both stupid and wasteful. In the case of Ken, his love is abundant. As for his dedication to preservation and display, the burghers of the Smithsonian might do well to visit Ken and ask his advice on how to present strangely shaped and proportioned objects (and let's face it—brightwork is weird and polymorphous and that's why we love it). Indeed, brightwork is sculpture, and as with orthodox sculpture, brightwork has historical roots and many differing schools. But at its core, brightwork is about the delirious collision between pop culture, Detroit, the dream of automotive escape, as well as that part of us that believes that the future can be seen as a better place owing to the cleverness of technology.

Aside from its formal beauty, brightwork will also belt you in the gut with its concentrated sense of optimism, and its largely mid-twentieth-century sense of unalloyed pleasure in the act of driving. Each piece also evokes period-specific aesthetic and culural resonance, and such Big Three boardroom imaginings as: "Don, the public's going crazy for rockets—put the biggest rocket you can on the hood of next year's model and do it now!"

I wasn't the least bit surprised when Ken told me he was doing a book on brightwork, and one would be hard-pressed to locate anybody more capable of doing the job. Most of all he's . . . well, he's just crazy about the darn things! And that's what makes for a good anything—a good collection, a good emblem from a 1955 Studebaker, and, in this particular case, a good and thorough book. Read on!

DOUGLAS COUPLAND
Vancouver
August 1999

INTRODUCTION

I can identify the very moment when my fascination with automotive ornaments began. I was visiting a friend who had moved recently to Los Angeles. Having decided that he needed a cool California car, he had settled on a cherry (color and condition) '55 Chrysler Windsor. While admiring the rakish lines, I was struck by a marvelous piece of sculpture that adorned the hood—a stylish, almost muscular eagle about to blast off into the wild blue yonder. "Gee, what a great-looking hood ornament, Scott!," I ventured, little realizing that I was about to embark on an acquisition spree that made my other collecting interests pale by comparison.

I soon came to realize that vintage cars, especially those made in the USA, were festooned with beautiful embellishments. Masterpieces of graphic design, emblems, script, nameplates, horn buttons, hubcaps, and sideflashes adorned the cars, front and back, side to side, inside and out. To be sure, there are many examples of awkward, incomprehensible designs on already ugly autos, but the hunt for aesthetically pleasing artifacts became a challenge I simply could not resist!

This book is an overview of collectible chrome auto parts. Some of the cars sporting these chrome bits are still cruising the turnpikes; most are pitted and rusting in scrap yards and on farms. These pieces are presented in isolation, unattached to the autos they decorated. This approach highlights their intrinsic aesthetic value, not their original function as mere automotive embellishments. The ornaments on these cars were, by their very nature, subordinate to the whole—in this case, the car they adorn. But what real purpose does this chrome serve, and why was so much time and effort expended to produce and place it on those massive automotive sculptures? The answer lies at the very heart of their appeal.

The Origins of American Automotive Style

Henry Ford didn't invent the automobile, but by creating the assembly line he made what had been affordable only by the rich available to common people (cars in any color, as the slogan went, as long as it's black). Ford was so cost-conscious, he even had subcontractors supply parts in wooden crates of specific dimensions so the wood could be used as floorboards in the Model T.

After World War I, cars went from novelty to necessity almost overnight. By the late twenties, sales were booming, but the automobile was still essentially three boxes with wheels. The first box housed the motor, the second the passengers, and the third luggage. The radiator was stuck on the front, and the headlamps bolted to the fenders. This arrangement worked just fine, but it was ugly and inefficient at the higher speeds being achieved by the introduction of what was to become a standard power plant: the V8 engine.

In the twenties, the sufficiently wealthy could buy the mechanics of a car—chassis, wheels, and an engine—then have the coachwork done by a custom outfit. Harley Earl and his father ran a custom business in California with great success. Hollywood stars lined up to buy the runabouts the Earls handcrafted. Harley's work was noticed by Detroit, and he was summoned by Alfred P. Sloane, president of General Motors, to try his hand at designing new cars.

Sloane's own research indicated that in the minds of the public styling ranked first in automotive importance, automatic transmissions second, and high-compression engines third. That was the ticket: looks, convenience, and speed. General Motors' engineers had already nailed down the last two, the first was now up to Harley Earl. He rose to the occasion, creating production cars as beautiful as one-off customs. At GM he started the Art and Colour [sic] department, which would revolutionize the look of not just GM's line, but all American automobiles.

Earl realized that the look and feel of a car, its "styling," was as important as its mechanical attributes. He knew that glamor could be marketed just as well as any other feature. Beginning by sculpting the mock-ups of new cars in clay, he abandoned the idea that form follows function and introduced design for its own sake. He said that his entire career was dedicated to making cars longer and lower. Earl invented the concept of the Dream Car, a vehicle so far ahead of its time it might never be built. But Dream Cars contained ideas that would appear in subsequent models: a fender, a bumper, perhaps an entire interior. Those features that made it into production were know as MAYA, an acronym for Most Advanced Yet Acceptable. He knew not to appeal to buyers solely on the basis of the freshness of the new look, but also to create a vague displeasure with existing models, thus ensuring repeat business. But as industrial designer Henry Dreyfuss observed, "We must be able to anticipate the public's desires, yet guard against being too far ahead." Earl called his doctrine "Dynamic Obsolescence," telling his designers to "go all the way, then back off."

Earl eliminated useful but old-fashioned notions like running boards, then blended fenders, trunks, and headlights into cohesive forms. The result was sleek, streamlined, and purpose-ful. By World War II, Earl had revolutionized the look and feel of American autos and trig-gered an immediate response from other man-ufacturers. Brilliant designers followed his bold lead: Raymond Loewy had a long and success-ful association with Studebaker; Virgil Exner revitalized Chrysler; and Gordon Buerig styled the exquisite 1936 Cord, which was named by the Museum of Modern Art as one of the greatest examples of industrial design of this century, and is thought by many to be the most beautiful car ever created.

Early in the war, a GM facility was turned over to the government to produce fighter planes. One of the planes, the Lockheed Lightning, impressed Earl and his design team. The plane's twin tails and vertical control surfaces intrigued Earl; he would use the concept to change the face of American automobile design for years to come. Those fins first appeared, tentatively, on the 1948 Cadillac.

11

They proceeded to grow and grow, reaching their apotheosis a decade later on the fabulous 1959 models. Resembling a pair of shark's dorsal fins slicing through traffic, they made the back of the car as interesting as the front. People paid attention. Everyone else jumped aboard the fin-wagon, some going as far as to suggest that they actually gave lateral stability to the car. But Earl knew that it was really a case of that sincerest form of flattery.

Though they took an entire decade to develop, the fins disappeared within a couple of years, as did most of the distinctive designs that gave American cars their character. Earl's successor, Bill Mitchell, complained that by the late sixties cars "all look alike— I have to read the goddamn badges to know what they are!" The lack of individual style and ornamentation was to blame.

What happened, and why did it happen so fast?

A prime factor was competition from foreign manufacturers, specifically the Volkswagen Beetle. The Bug's success flew in the face of Detroit's doctrine of planned obsolescence: It was a timeless, utterly novel design that only needed fine-tuning from one year to the next, not a complete and costly overhaul. That little car's phenomenal success had the Big Three U.S. manufacturers scrambling to compete by producing cheap, featureless vehicles. Style was sacrificed on the altar of economy. The only exceptions were the exceptional Corvette and the first pony car, Ford's Mustang.

The change reflected the American cultural landscape: people were growing more impressed with performance than appearance. Status was measured in cubic-inch displacement and not fin size or the surface area of chrome. But even that was short-lived: inflation, the oil crisis, pollution controls, and increased pressure from German and Japanese imports spelled the end of Muscle Car mania. What was left was not a pretty sight, literally.

The Big Three had also thrived on intergenerational owner loyalty. But it was to become an unstable crutch in the sixties and seventies. People were no longer content to buy whatever Detroit threw at them just because it still had that familiar logo. Previously, owners changed the make of their car to mark a change in their status or prestige. But as buyers became more knowledgeable, blind owner loyalty no longer ruled the showrooms.

Detroit also learned early on that women are a tremendously important factor in marketing. Men still bought most cars, but the decisions were often decisively swayed by women. Manufacturers discovered that while men reacted emotionally to a car's appeal, a women responded more rationally. Conveniences like power steering, brakes, and adjustable seats were therefore touted prominently in sales literature beside horsepower, compression ratios, and acceleration curves.

Marshall McLuhan observed that old technologies are often retrieved as art objects; the automobile and its adornments are no exception. Automotive museums began springing up shortly after WWII. Today, many collections present the cars as works of sculpture that will never again move under their own power. And displayed with these static former conveyances are hood ornaments, horn buttons, emblems, and script, those shiny touchstones that recall a halcyon time when style counted for something.

Art Meets Commerce & Vice Versa

From the turn of the century until World War II, numerous artistic theories influenced designers and artists alike. Futurism, vorticism, suprematism, constructivism, cubism, precisionism, Vienna Secession, Vienna Werkstatte, Bauhaus, Jugendstil, de Stijl, international style, liberty style, WPA style, arts and crafts, art nouveau, art moderne, and of course, art deco shaped the look and feel of industrial design from packaging to Packards. The central idea was to eliminate anything obtrusive or inefficient, rendering what remained dynamic, functional, and beautiful.

The resulting explosion of exquisite design has, as far as I'm concerned, yet to be superseded. Unfortunately, the art quickly became unaffordable and the essentially disposable artifacts disappeared from the cultural landscape. That is, of course, what makes tracking down prewar brightwork such a challenge, and such a pleasure when you stumble across something. Fortunately for the student of style, there are still plenty of the automobiles that these things were attached to, but this is cold comfort for the brightwork collector who can often only look and yearn. There are also plenty of sales brochures, advertisements in period magazines, and other promotional material.

World War II forever changed American buying habits. The war years were difficult, and conspicuous consumerism was our reward. Automotive styling also changed dramatically. Bigger was definitely better. Cars in the fifties had more of everything: more chrome, more glass, more horsepower, more weight, length, and width. As the surface area grew, so, too, did the need for more brightwork to identify the make.

As brightwork proliferated, new motifs reflected advances in technology. Rocketships, jet planes, and other atomic age icons abounded until late in the decade, when Detroit decided that these were extraneous. The hood ornaments went first, then the nifty horn buttons, and finally the inventive script and emblems. By the mid-sixties, all that was left were plasticplaques that spelled out the maker's name in a cold, sans-serif face. A couple of snazzy models bucked the trend, but by the Summer of Love in 1967 it was all over.

Of late, Detroit stylists have reached all the way back to the thirties to retrieve corporate emblems to stick on their latest com-puterized and style-challenged cars. But the effect is distinctly ad hoc and fools no one. It's been a long time since a kid could identify a car from a block away . . . or cared.

The research for this book has been a fascinating experience. Beyond the obvious facts as to what model year and make of car these artifacts came from, precious little else can be found about their design origins. Obviously, they are inspired by the cultural aesthetic in

vogue at the time they were made, but who actually made them?

Determining the designers of most American hood ornaments has been next to impossible. The only designs with any kind of personal profile are the two made for Nash by *Esquire* magazine's pinup artist George Petty. His first highly-stylized goddess adorned the hood of the 1950 Nash Airflyte, but did little to distract attention from the car's bathtub form. The second ornament, done two years later, was rather more repre-sentational and appealing. Both were engraved with his distinctive signature.

Most of the other brightwork in this collection was probably designed and produced by anonymous employees of the various manufac-turers. Research turned up a few photos of guys carving emblem masters out of solid brass or mahogany, but they were identified only as "styling division workers."

The Fabulous Finale

The hood ornaments that came with a new car were called factory mascots, as distinct from accessory mascots that were purchased to personalize a car. Accessory mascots ranged from dirt-cheap tin alloy items to fabulously expensive crystals by Lalique. Some were absolutely spectacular, and included lights that became more intense as the car accelerated. All of the brightwork in this volume was either standard equipment that came with the basic car or deluxe accessories added as a buyer would air conditioning or a bigger engine.

The fact that these objects are all from U.S. auto manufacturers means that the most famous hood ornament of all isn't included in this collection: the Rolls Royce's lovely "Spirit of Ecstasy." Rolls and Jaguar are the only marques that still have a mascot to this day. We know a great deal about not just the artist who designed and sculpted the Spirit, but about the model as well. The former is one Charles Sykes, a well-regarded turn-of-the-century artist; the latter was Lord Montagu's secretary, Eleanor Thornton.

The mascot was made to address the appalling habit people had of accessorizing their Rollers with tasteless mascots—one chap apparently had his stainless steel hip joint mounted on the radiator cap and inscribed, "A Loyal Supporter"! The desire to individualize one's means of transport did not excuse this disregard for the dignity of the Rolls, at least not as far as the Board of Directors was concerned. And so the Spirit of Ecstasy was born, and happily remains with us to this day.

Makers invariably chose images of speed, strength, and elegance for their ornaments. Birds of prey, wild game, and hunting dogs were just part of the veritable menagerie cast and chromed over the years. As previously mentioned, spaceships and aircraft were also very popular, as were other conveyances such

as trains and ships.The most distinctive and
long-lived icons were Pontiac's Indian heads,
which were utilized not just on the hood but in
every other conceivable location including
horn buttons and emblems. Mercury's god of
speed also enjoyed design longevity.

Certainly the goddesses are the most lovely and
appealing of all the ornaments in the market-
place and in this book. Although many manufacturers adorned the hoods of their cars with
winged women, Cadillac, DeSoto, and
Nash crafted absolutely stunning
female forms. Sensuous and
bursting with vitality,
they epitomized the marriage
of power and sex appeal that is
emblematic of the American automobile.
Some were actually useful, hiding hood-release
latches beneath their flowing robes. GM surely
knew what it was doing when it required a
Cadillac owner to grasp the goddess firmly, then
pull upwards until she pointed her glistening
face heavenward. Only then could the hood
be lifted, revealing the throbbing power plant
beneath. It was another world, one we can
now only catch glimpses of, reflected in the
compound curves of these scintillating *objets d'arts*.

1932 DESOTO

HOOD ORNAMENTS

The most obvious and striking elements of automotive corporate identity are the chrome sculptures that proudly adorned the hoods of every automaker until the mid-fifties. By then, concern was already growing that they were too big and heavy, potentially dangerous, and cost too much to manufacture. In the early sixties, Ralph Nader's book *Unsafe at Any Speed* increased concern about auto safety. Few people wanted to have several pounds of lethal (albeit beautiful) chromed potmetal hurtling through their windscreen, and so the mascots disappeared. Farewell, lovely ladies, svelte beasts, and phallic spaceships. Hello lackluster crests.

In addition to the sensuous goddesses of speed and light, also presented here are practically every Pontiac ornament from 1935, when it received a dramatic art deco makeover (prior to this it had been strictly representational and rather dull), until its startling transformation into a jet fighter in 1954, and finally its figurative decapitation and segue into a simple boomerang a couple of years later. Other progressions of note are Oldsmobile's rocketship and Chevrolet's eagle, which also became a bizarre aircraft hybrid before disappearing completely by the mid-fifties.

1934 PONTIAC V8

1934–1935 BUICK

1940 PACKARD SUPER 8

1948–1951 PACKARD DELUXE

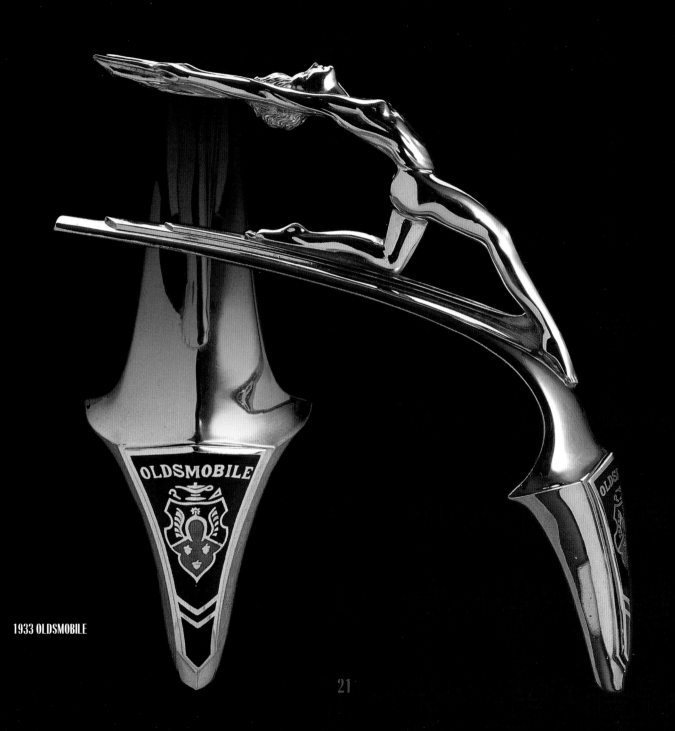

1933 OLDSMOBILE

21

Ra, the Egyptian sun god, eagerly anticipates the road ahead.

1926–1935 STUTZ

1928 BUICK

1927 BUICK

1929–1931 CHEVROLET

1931–1932 PLYMOUTH

23

At the 1956 New York Automobile Show, DeSoto highlighted a living hood ornament years after the chrome ones had disappeared from their cars.

1935–1936, 1932, 1933 DESOTO

1937 DESOTO

1939 DESOTO

1941 DESOTO

1942–1948 DESOTO

The only artist with the clout to sign his designs, George Petty is shown at right hard at work on one of his two Nash ornaments.

1948 NASH

1952 NASH

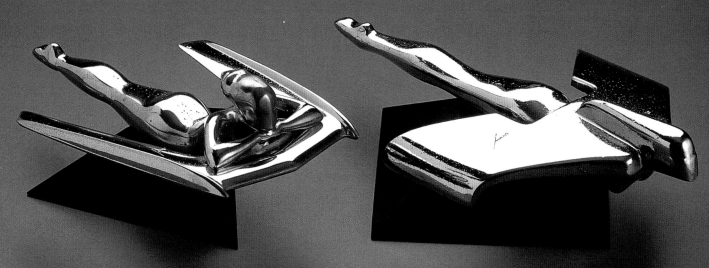

1953–1954 NASH

1949–1951 NASH

1930—1932 CADILLAC

1933—1936 CADILLAC

1936 CADILLAC V8

1933–1934 CADILLAC V8

1942 CADILLAC

1941 CADILLAC

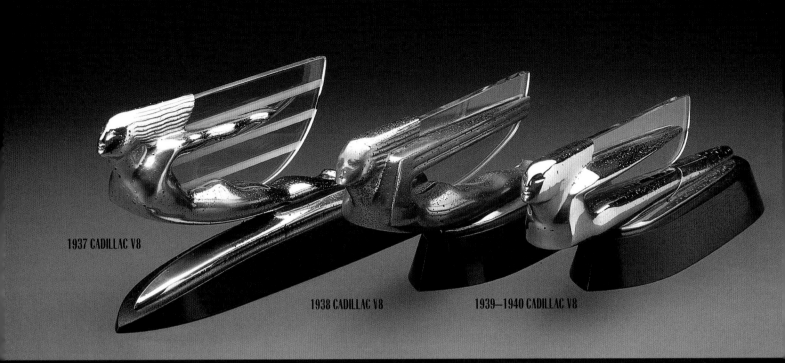

1937 CADILLAC V8

1938 CADILLAC V8

1939—1940 CADILLAC V8

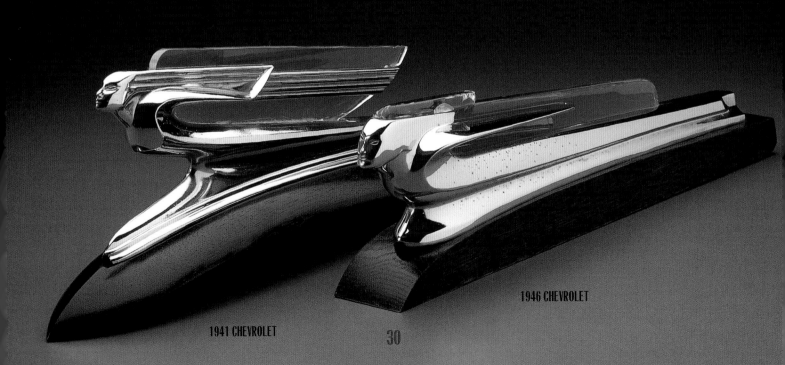

1941 CHEVROLET

1946 CHEVROLET

1948—1949 CADILLAC

1955 CADILLAC

1954 CADILLAC

1956 CADILLAC

These two highly stylized birds atop their radiator cap perches vied for customers' attention.

1934 CHEVROLET

1932–1934 STUDEBAKER

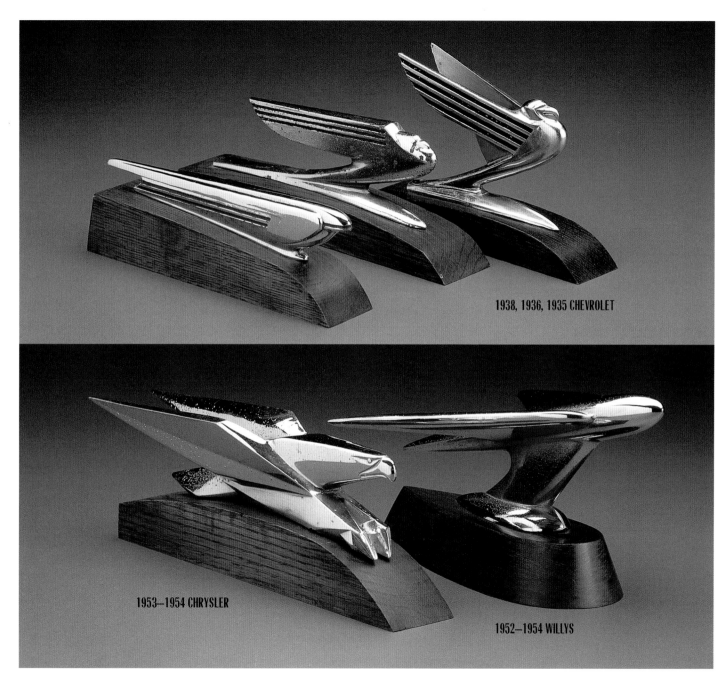

1938, 1936, 1935 CHEVROLET

1953–1954 CHRYSLER

1952–1954 WILLYS

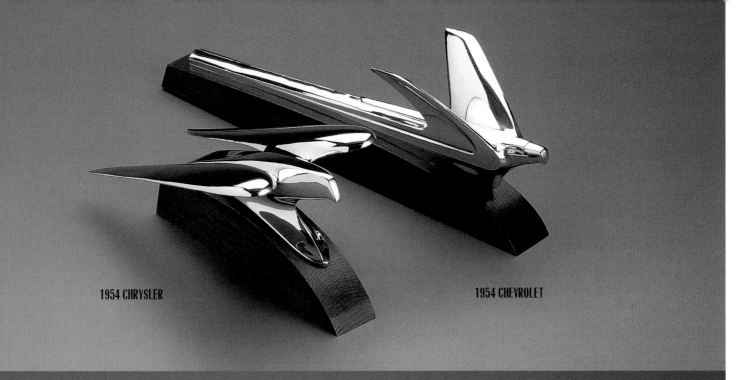

1954 CHRYSLER

1954 CHEVROLET

1954 CHEVROLET

1953–1954 CHEVROLET

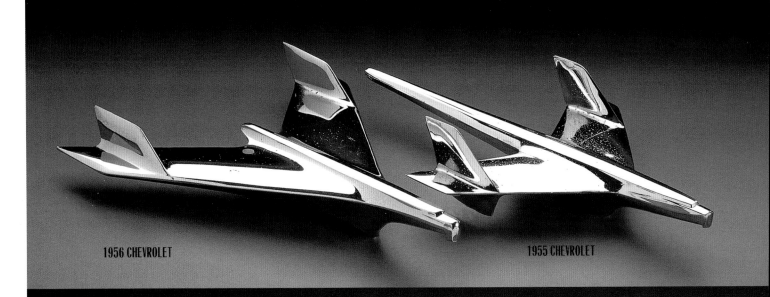

1956 CHEVROLET

1955 CHEVROLET

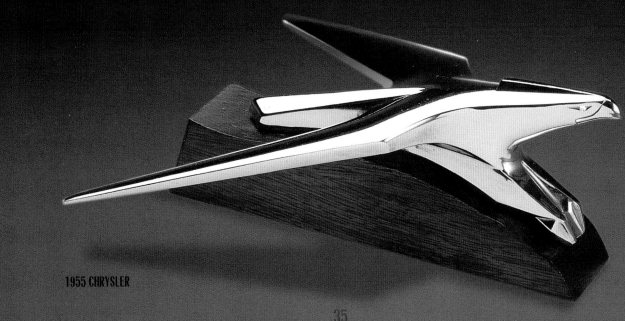

1955 CHRYSLER

1951—1952 CHRYSLER

1928 CHEVROLET

36

Ford showcased their products at the 1939—1940 New York World´s Fair, giving us a glimpse of the way the future might have been.

1946—1947, 1940—1941 & 1948, 1942 LINCOLN

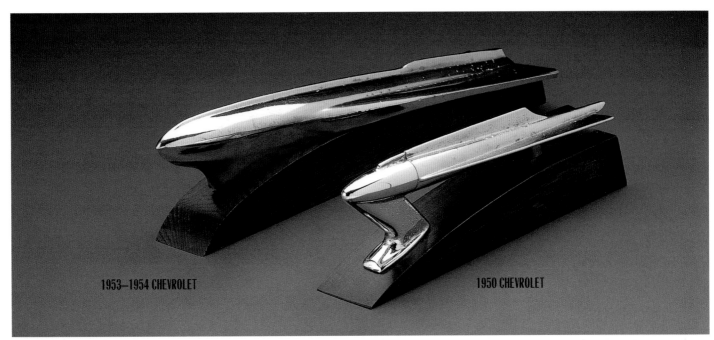

1953–1954 CHEVROLET   1950 CHEVROLET

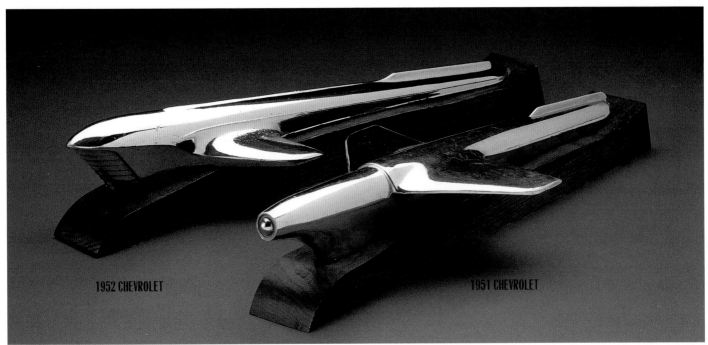

1952 CHEVROLET   1951 CHEVROLET

1940, 1937 CHRYSLER

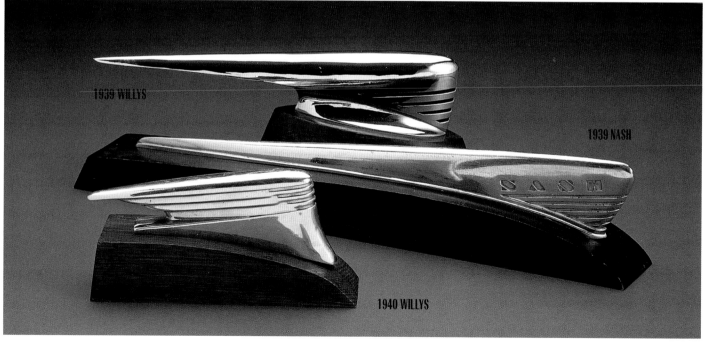

1939 WILLYS

1939 NASH

1940 WILLYS

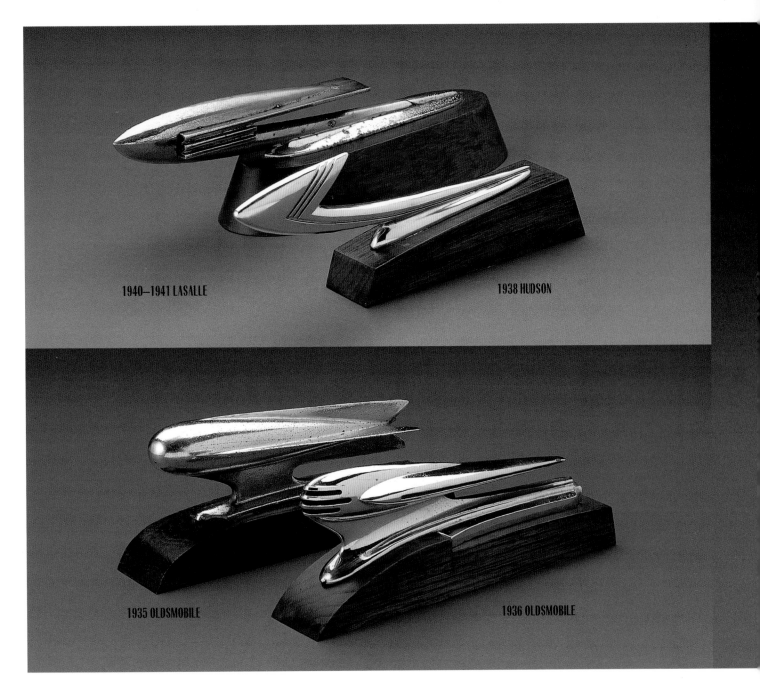

1940–1941 LASALLE

1938 HUDSON

1935 OLDSMOBILE

1936 OLDSMOBILE

Flash Gordon or Buck Rogers would surely have been proud to pilot this particular ornament.

1935–1936 HUPMOBILE

The streamline style not only improved aerodynamic flow in planes, trains, and automobiles, but it also married art and technology.

1941 CHEVROLET

1938 BUICK

1937 BUICK

1950 FORD

1949 FORD

1940 OLDSMOBILE

1951–1953 PACKARD

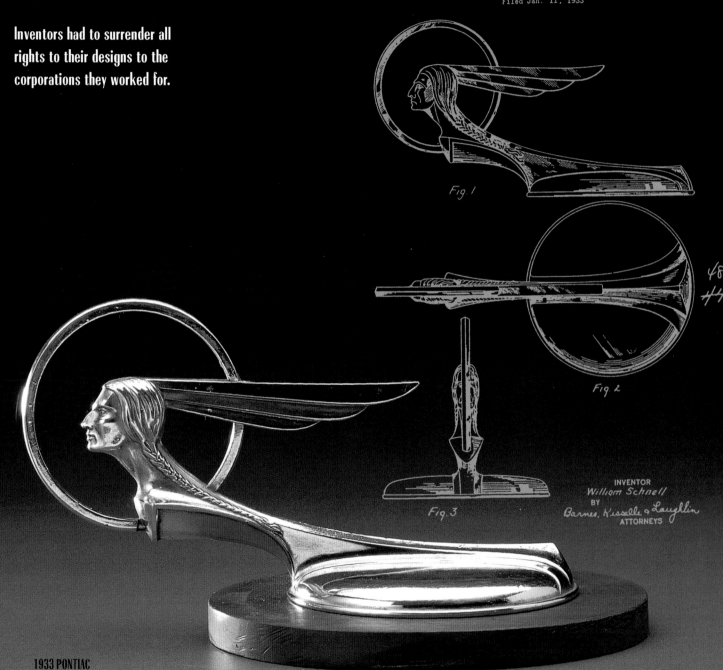

Inventors had to surrender all rights to their designs to the corporations they worked for.

March 14, 1933.   W. SCHNELL   Des. 89,453

AUTOMOBILE RADIATOR ORNAMENT OR SIMILAR ARTICLE

Filed Jan. 11, 1933

Fig. 1

Fig. 2

Fig. 3

INVENTOR
William Schnell
BY
Barnes, Kisselle & Laughlin
ATTORNEYS

1933 PONTIAC

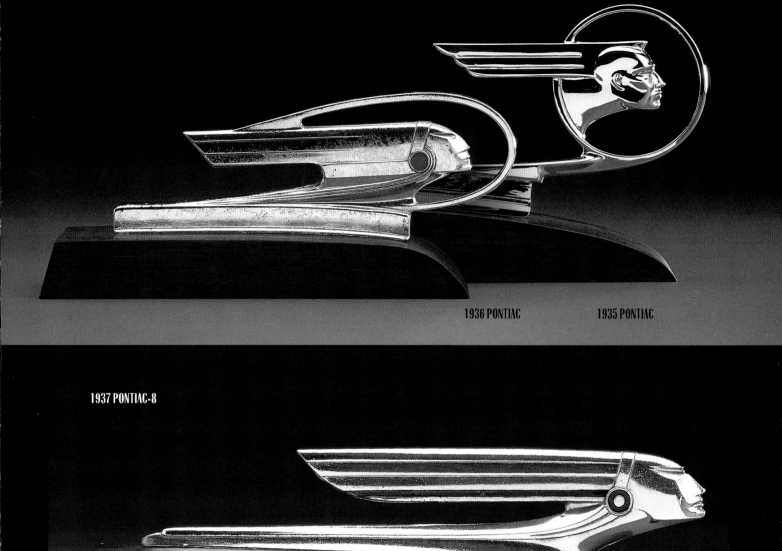

1936 PONTIAC   1935 PONTIAC

1937 PONTIAC-8

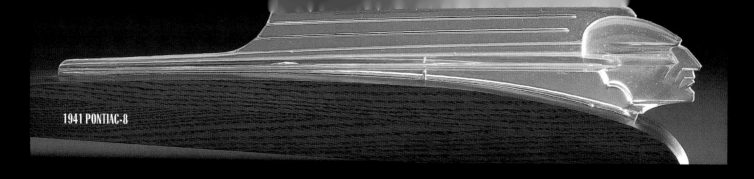

1941 PONTIAC-8

A number of manufacturers, including Pontiac, turned to plastic for their hood ornaments in order to save on strategic materials during the 1941 and 1942 model years.

1941 PONTIAC

1942 PONTIAC

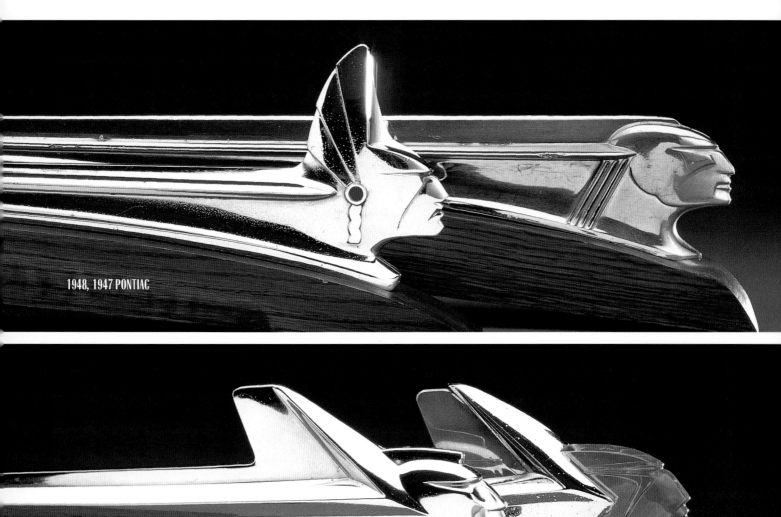

1948, 1947 PONTIAC

1952 PONTIAC, 1952 PONTIAC DELUXE

48

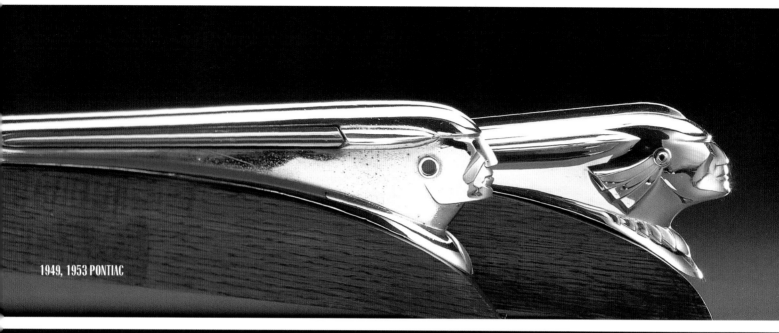

1949, 1953 PONTIAC

1948, 1946 PONTIAC

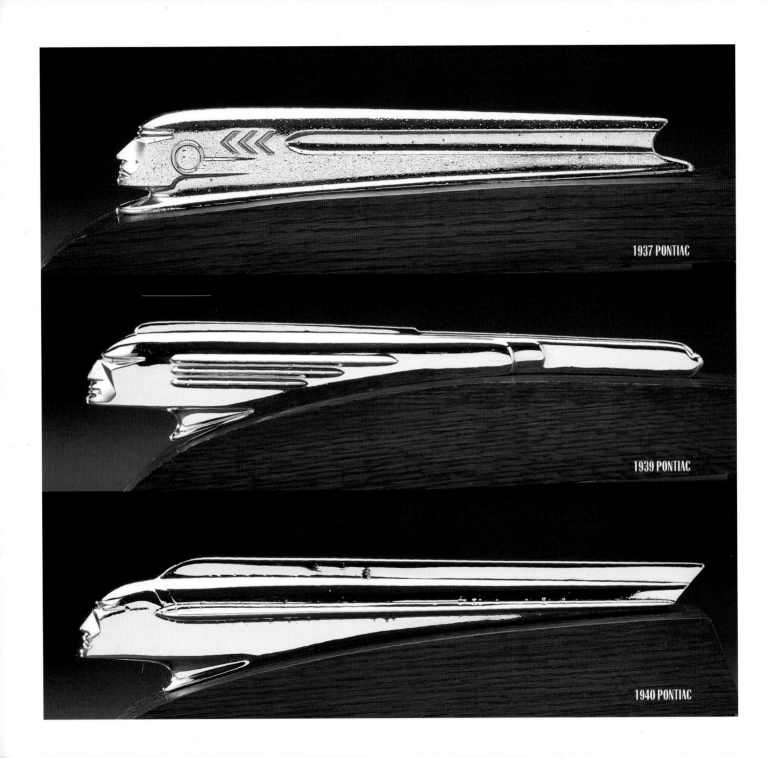

1937 PONTIAC

1939 PONTIAC

1940 PONTIAC

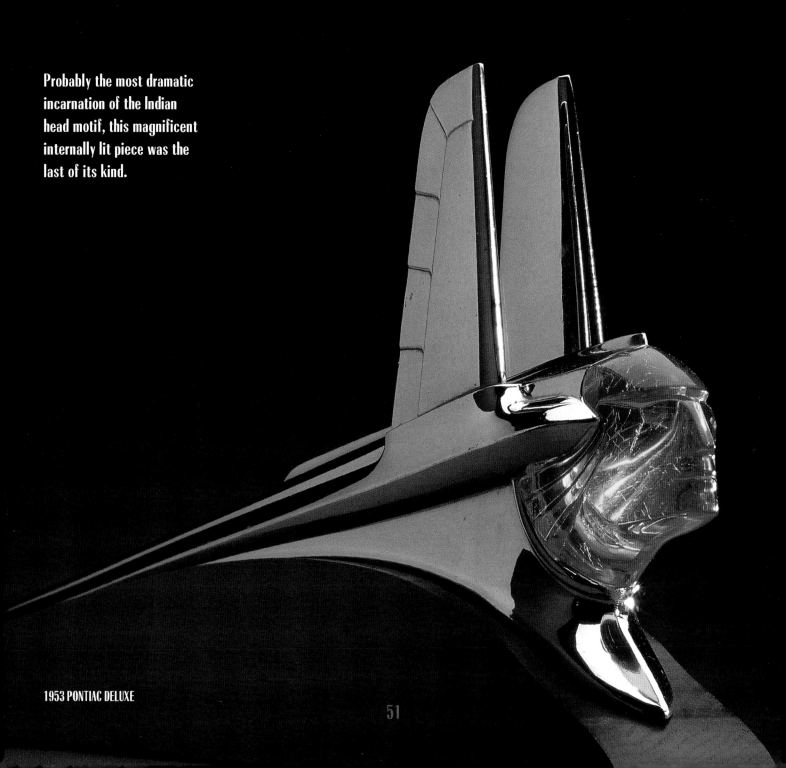

Probably the most dramatic incarnation of the Indian head motif, this magnificent internally lit piece was the last of its kind.

1953 PONTIAC DELUXE

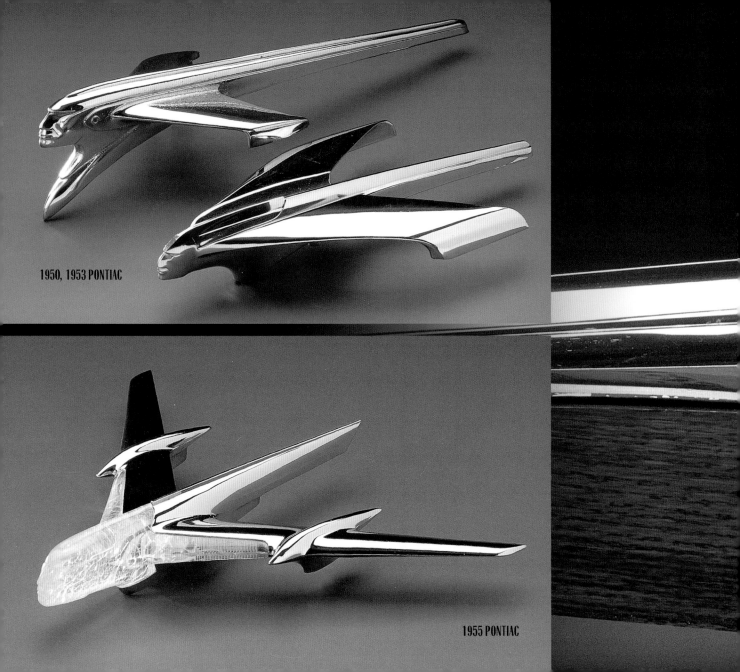

1950, 1953 PONTIAC

1955 PONTIAC

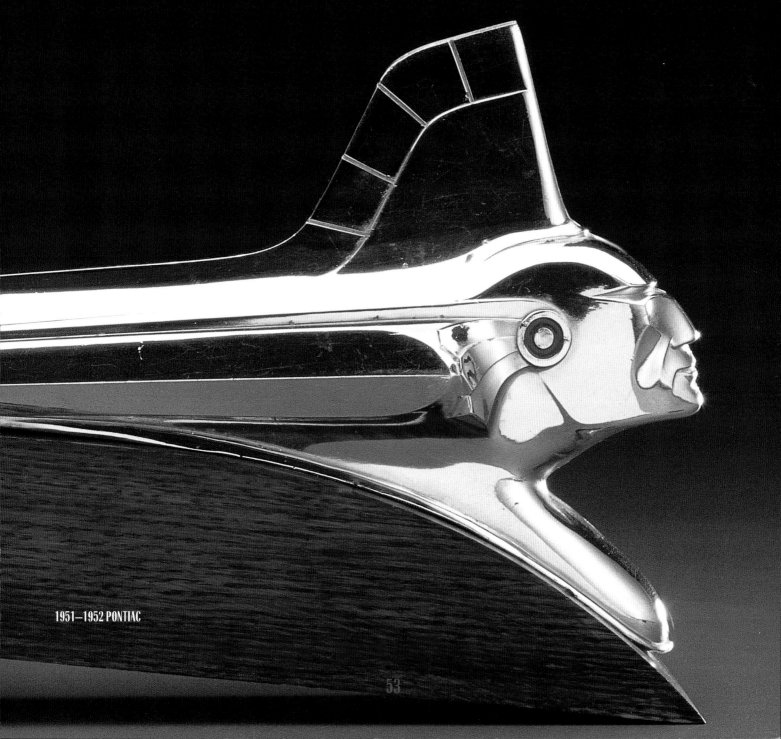

1951–1952 PONTIAC

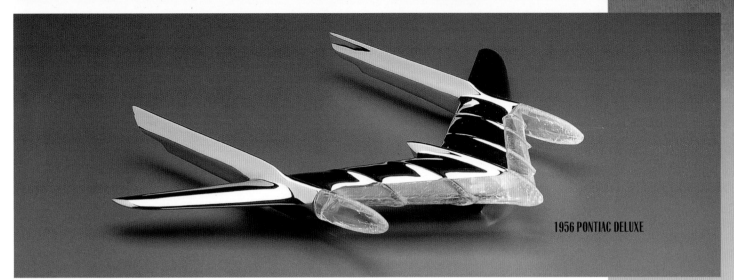

1956 PONTIAC DELUXE

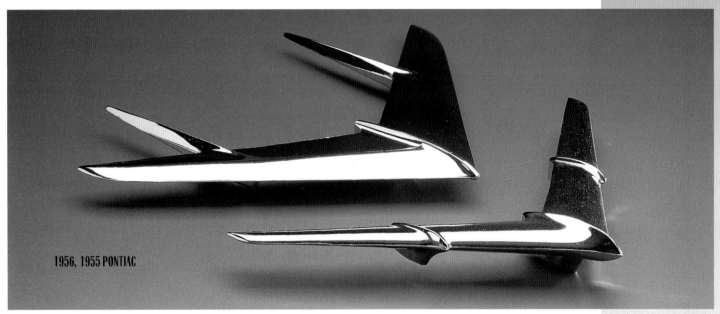

1956, 1955 PONTIAC

1954 PONTIAC

The astounding post-war advances in aerospace technology were noticed by Detroit, which did its utmost to capitalize on the public's fascination with aircraft that flew farther, higher, and faster, like this 1949 Northrop YB-49 Flying Wing.

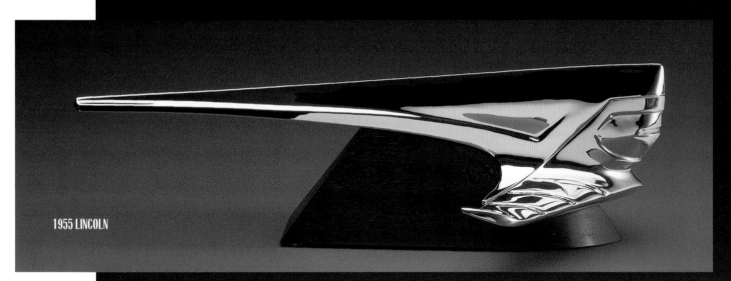

1955 LINCOLN

1938–1939 GRAHAM

1955–1956 LINCOLN TRUNK

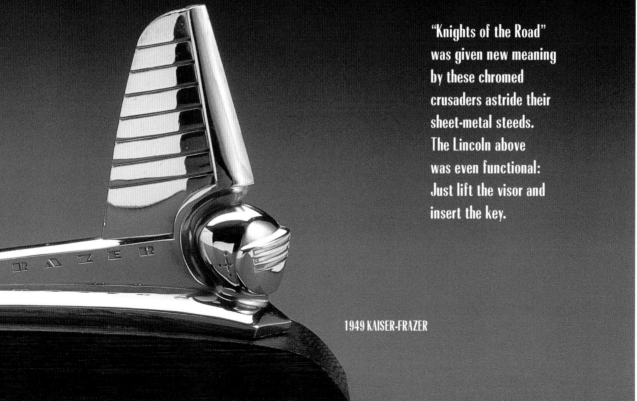

1949 KAISER-FRAZER

"Knights of the Road"
was given new meaning
by these chromed
crusaders astride their
sheet-metal steeds.
The Lincoln above
was even functional:
Just lift the visor and
insert the key.

1934—1939 LINCOLN

1937—1938 MACK

1954 FORD   1950 FORD   1951 CHEVROLET

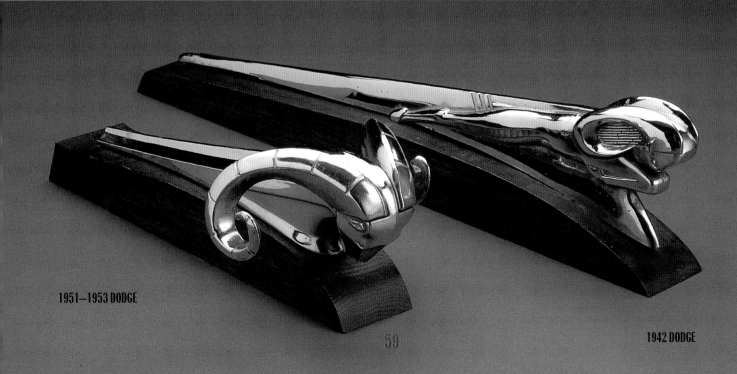

1951–1953 DODGE

1942 DODGE

1957 DODGE

1940 CHEVROLET

1946 CHEVROLET

1947–1948 CHEVROLET

Obviously delighted to
be bolted to your hood,
explorer Hernando
DeSoto's face lit up
when you turned on
the headlights.

1933 ESSEX

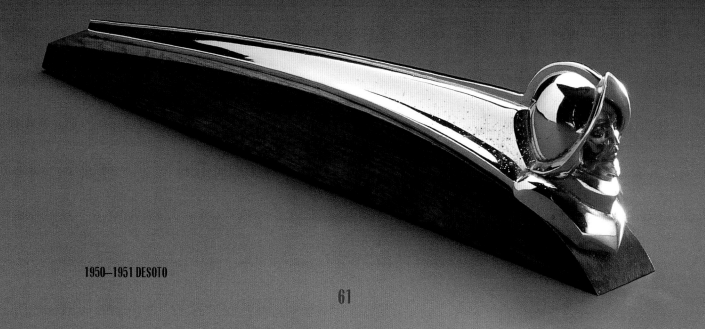

1950–1951 DESOTO

61

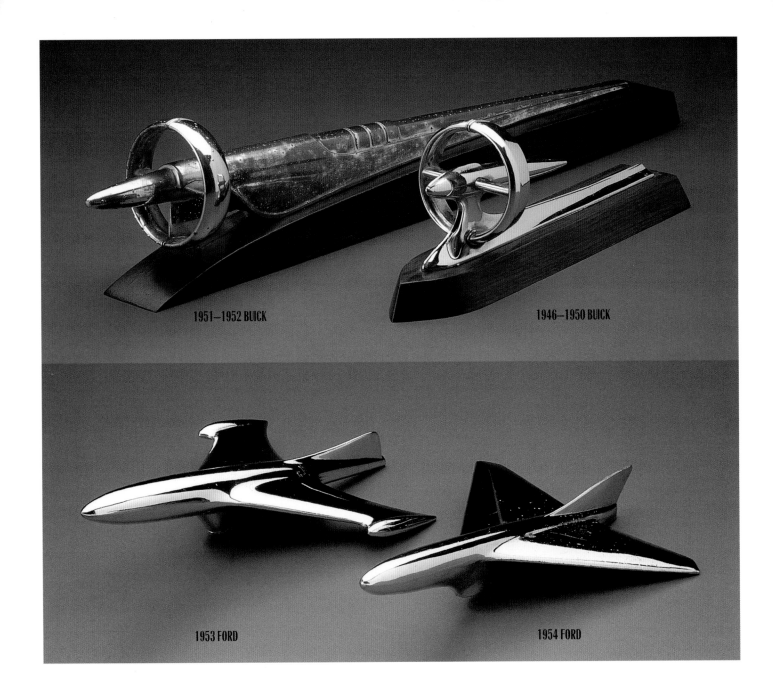

1951–1952 BUICK

1946–1950 BUICK

1953 FORD

1954 FORD

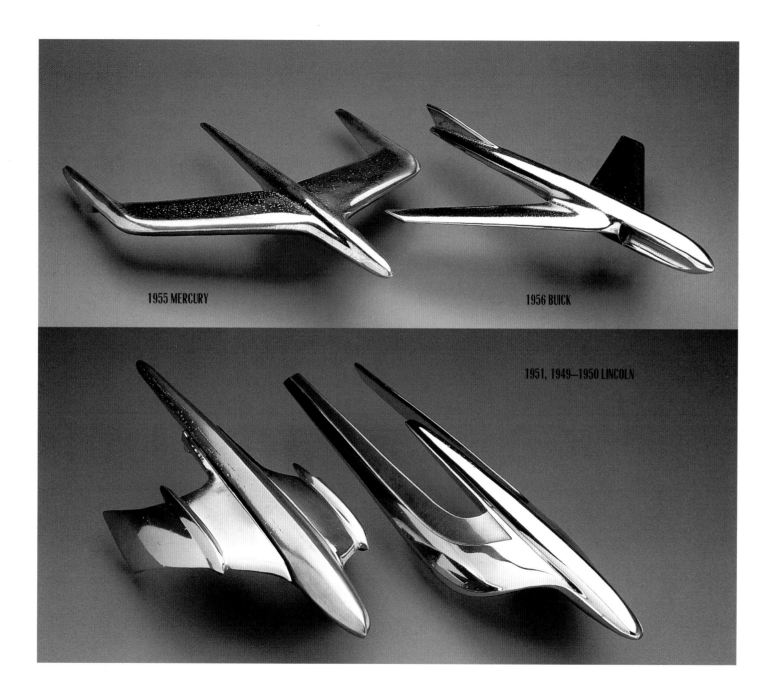

1955 MERCURY

1956 BUICK

1951, 1949–1950 LINCOLN

Rockets captured the public's imagination as symbols of both exploration and Cold War military might.

1953—1954 OLDSMOBILE

1950 OLDSMOBILE

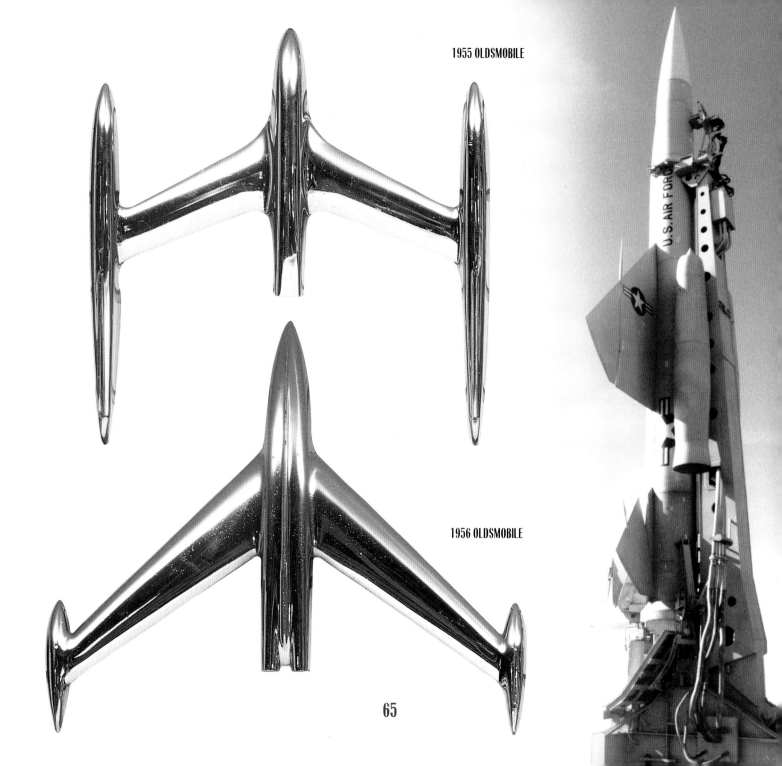

1955 OLDSMOBILE

1956 OLDSMOBILE

65

LATE-1940s PONTIAC

HORN BUTTONS

Horn buttons are the most functional of the objects in this book. Manufacturers were well aware that the big button you hit when someone cuts you off was an ideal place for a logo to remind drivers of the maker of their automobile. The circular format required a conscious effort on the part of the designers to come up with solutions for shoehorning their logo or mascot into this space.

The buttons had to be durable, too. Initially, manufacturers crafted the buttons out of enamelled metal that was bright and wore well. Later, the new plastics were utilized, including Bakelite, Lucite, and Plexiglas. The tough, transparent materials freed designers to incorporate many intricate elements into the piece. Throughout the fifties, complex designs flourished, particularly at Pontiac and Mercury, whose jewel-like busts of their namesakes floated just below the polished plastic surface. Sadly, by the late fifties and early sixties, the steering wheel had become as utilitarian as the rest of the car, and the horn button was replaced usually by a cheap, colorless moniker or the indented outline of a bugle.

Chief Pontiac´s noble visage, complete with
swept feathers and mohawk, graced GM´s
products from 1926 to 1955.

1950s PONTIAC

MID-1950s PONTIAC

70

LATE-1940s, EARLY-1950s PONTIAC

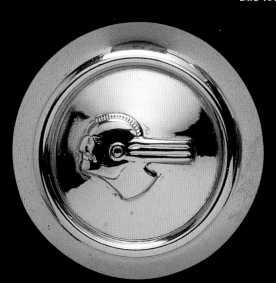

1950 PONTIAC   1949 PONTIAC

1959 PONTIAC

The horn button's standard circular shape ultimately gave way to freer, more expressive forms.

LATE-1940s   MONARCH

LATE-1960s CHEVROLET

Studebaker benefited enormously from famed industrial designer Raymond Loewy's credo of "Less is More."

LATE-1930s—1950s STUDEBAKER

MID-1950s MERCURY

76

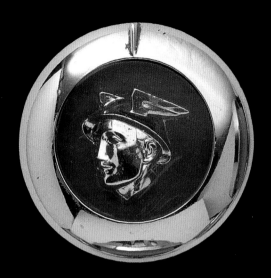

1950s MERCURY

1953 DESOTO

1951–1952 DESOTO

LATE-1950s PLYMOUTH

1957 DODGE

1949 LINCOLN

1950–1951 LINCOLN

1948 CHRYSLER

1949 CHRYSLER

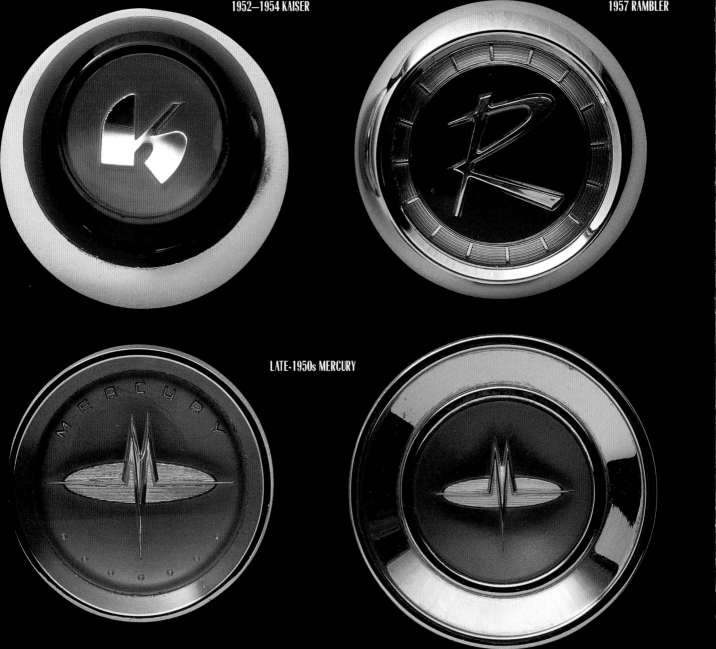

LATE-1950s MERCURY

Icons of Kaiser's shipbuilding and manufacturing enterprises ring their logo.

1952 KAISER

1949 BUICK

1954 MERCURY

1955 DESOTO

1950 PACKARD

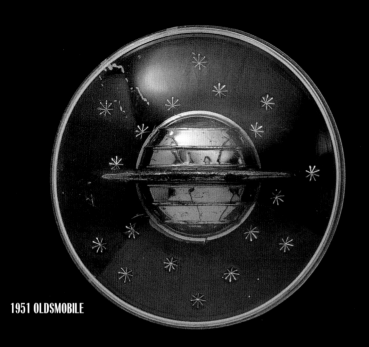

1951 OLDSMOBILE

1954 MERCURY

1957 STUDEBAKER

LATE-1950s STUDEBAKER

LATE-1950s CHEVROLET

LATE-1930s DODGE

LATE-1930s DODGE

85

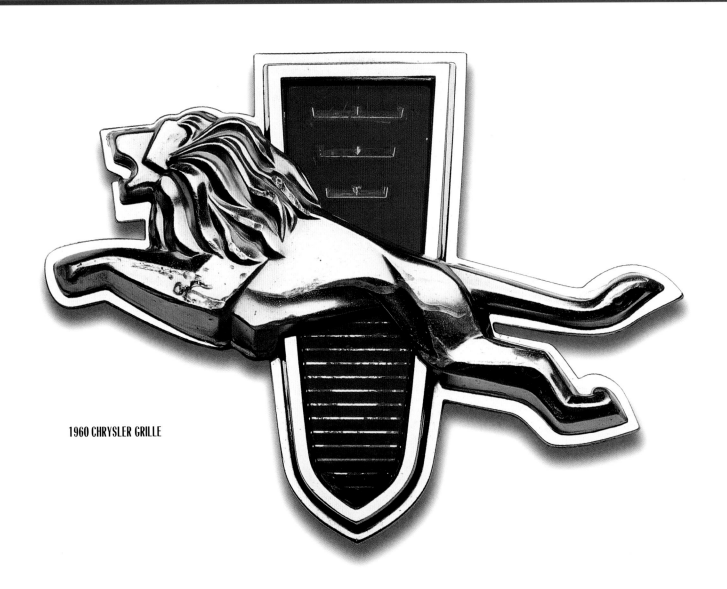

1960 CHRYSLER GRILLE

EMBLEMS

In the unlikely event that you (or your neighbor) forgot that you drove, say, a Royal Lancer, Chrysler placed shiny little logos practically everywhere. Other manufacturers did, too. At one point, there appeared to be a contest to see which maker could advertise more prominently. On the exterior, emblems perched above the bumper, and adorned the quarter panels, fenders, doors, hubcaps, and trunk latches. Inside, they decorated the glove box lid, dashboard, door panels, upholstery, sun visor—you name it, some manufacturer slapped an emblem onto it.

In the late twenties, the emblems were made of *champ levée*, a kind of enamelled bronze, but these costly items were soon replaced by poly-chromed potmetal and, eventually, plastic. While some are combinations of script and sculptural elements, others are pure design. They served no real practical purpose, but most were artfully designed.

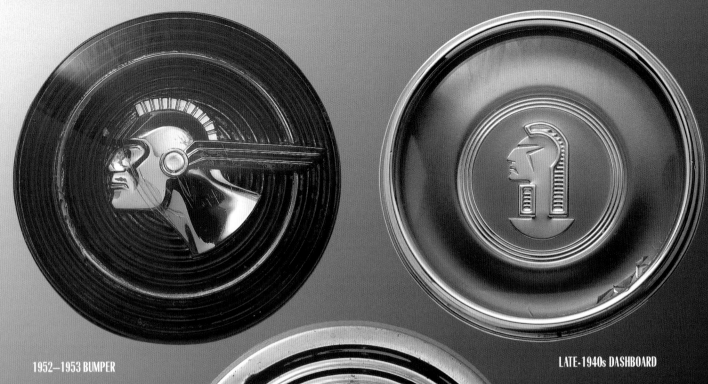

1952–1953 BUMPER

LATE-1940s DASHBOARD

LATE-1940s HUBCAP

1951–1953 PONTIAC REAR QUARTER PANEL

LATE-1930s,
LATE-1940s
PONTIAC

90

This solidly stylish
Pontiac was the
centerpiece of
the front bumper.

1948 PONTIAC BUMPER

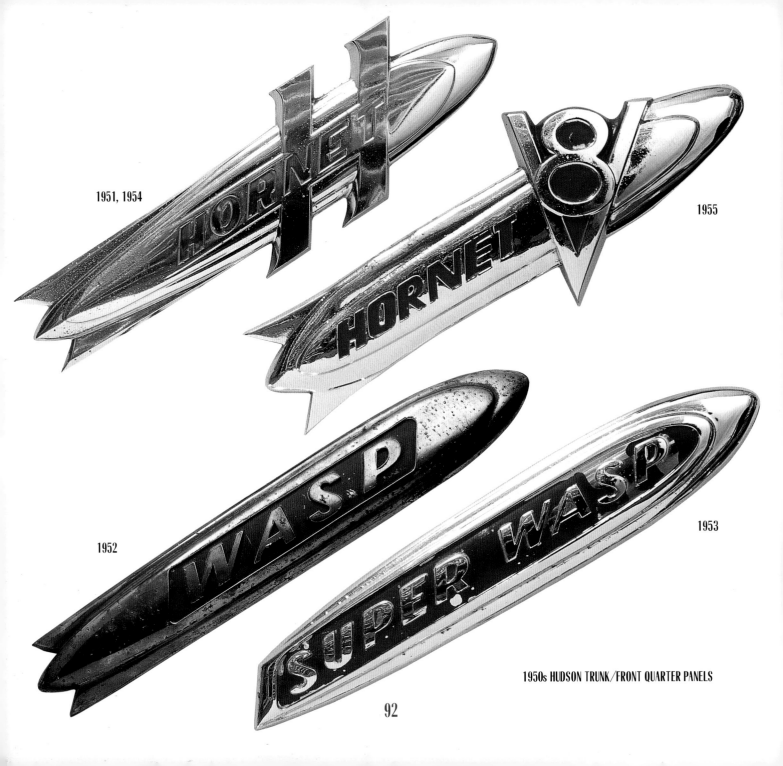

1951, 1954

1955

1952

1953

1950s HUDSON TRUNK/FRONT QUARTER PANELS

92

1950s METEOR

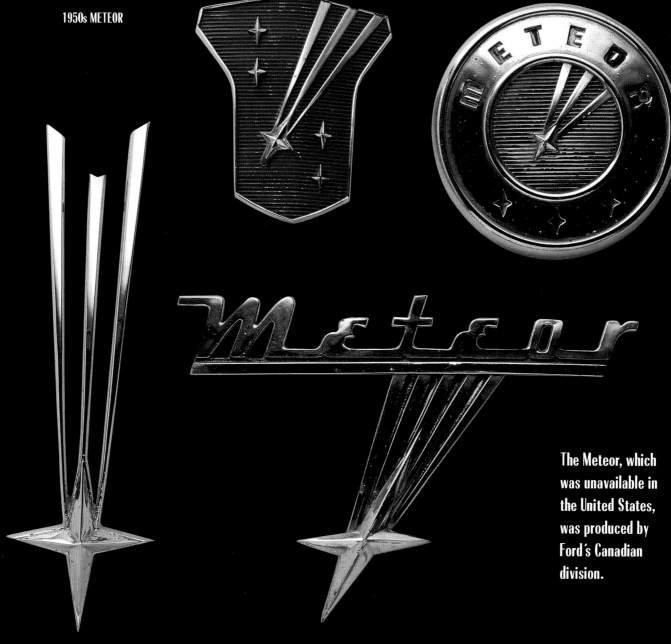

The Meteor, which was unavailable in the United States, was produced by Ford's Canadian division.

93

LATE-1940s OLDSMOBILE HUBCAP

EARLY-1950s OLDSMOBILE HOOD

94

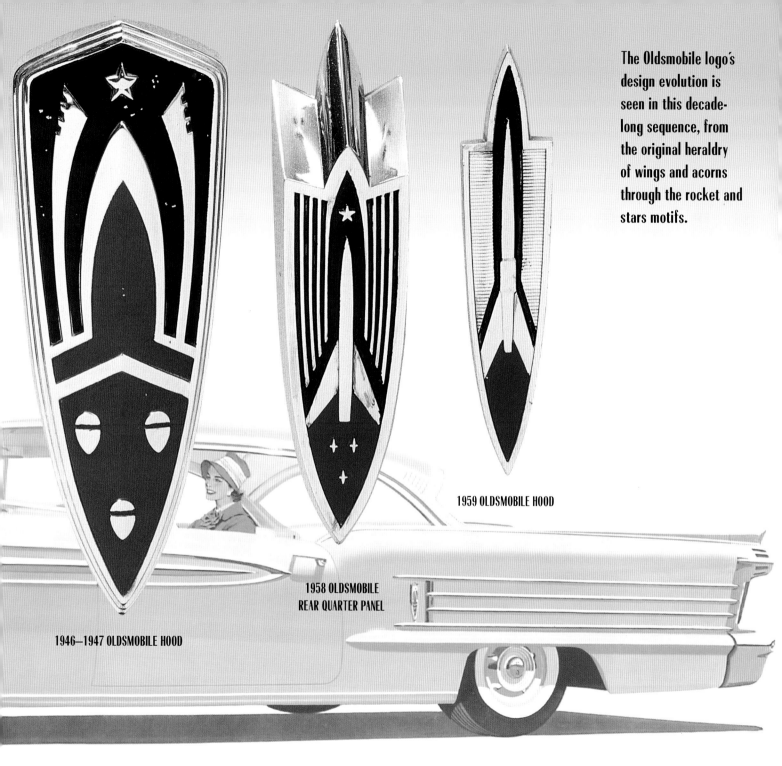

The Oldsmobile logo's design evolution is seen in this decade-long sequence, from the original heraldry of wings and acorns through the rocket and stars motifs.

1959 OLDSMOBILE HOOD

1958 OLDSMOBILE REAR QUARTER PANEL

1946–1947 OLDSMOBILE HOOD

LATE-1940s OLDSMOBILE HOOD

LATE-1940s DESOTO HOOD

1950 CHRYSLER HOOD

Personal heraldry was given
a corporate twist by Detroit.

LATE-1950s MONARCH HOOD

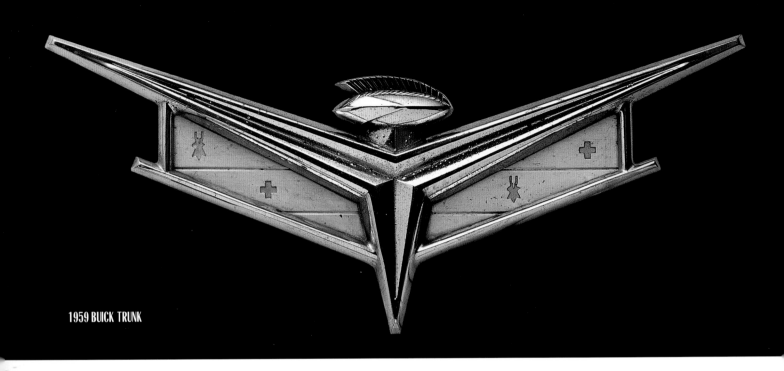

1959 BUICK TRUNK

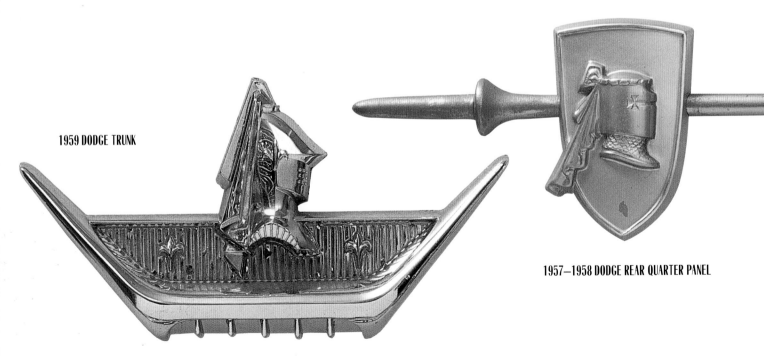

1959 DODGE TRUNK

1957—1958 DODGE REAR QUARTER PANEL

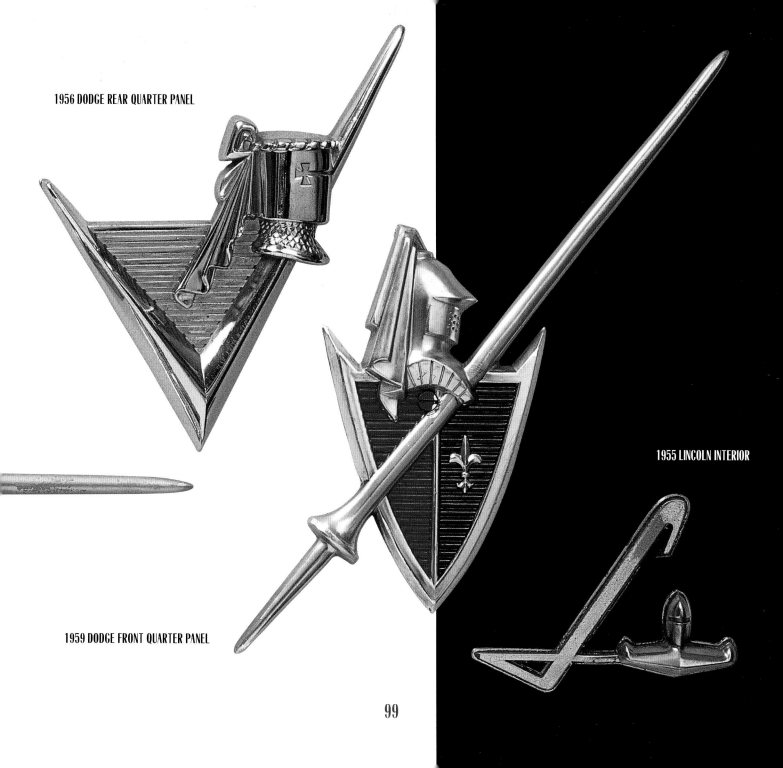

1956 DODGE REAR QUARTER PANEL

1955 LINCOLN INTERIOR

1959 DODGE FRONT QUARTER PANEL

99

LATE-1930s CHRYSLER HOOD

1941 CHRYSLER HOOD

LATE-1930s PLYMOUTH TRUNK

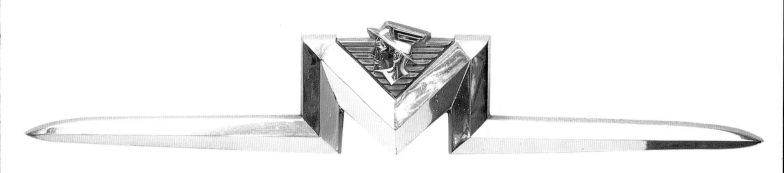

1956 MERCURY HOOD

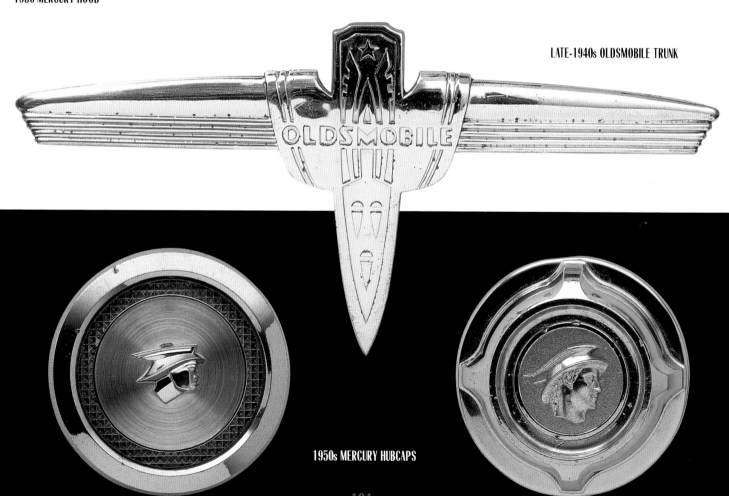

LATE-1940s OLDSMOBILE TRUNK

1950s MERCURY HUBCAPS

1925 HUPMOBILE GRILLE

1928 NASH GRILLE

1937 CORD FRONT BUMPER

LATE-1920s RICKENBACKER

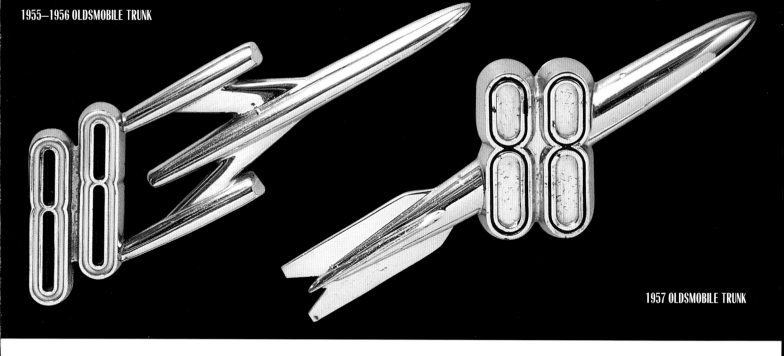

1955–1956 OLDSMOBILE TRUNK

1957 OLDSMOBILE TRUNK

1951–1952 BUICK FRONT QUARTER PANEL

1951–1952 BUICK SPECIAL FRONT QUARTER PANEL

103

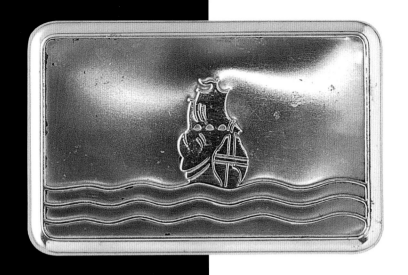

1930s PLYMOUTH DASHBOARD

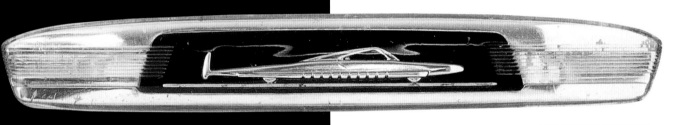

1954 MERCURY DASHBOARD

1940s HUDSON DASHBOARD

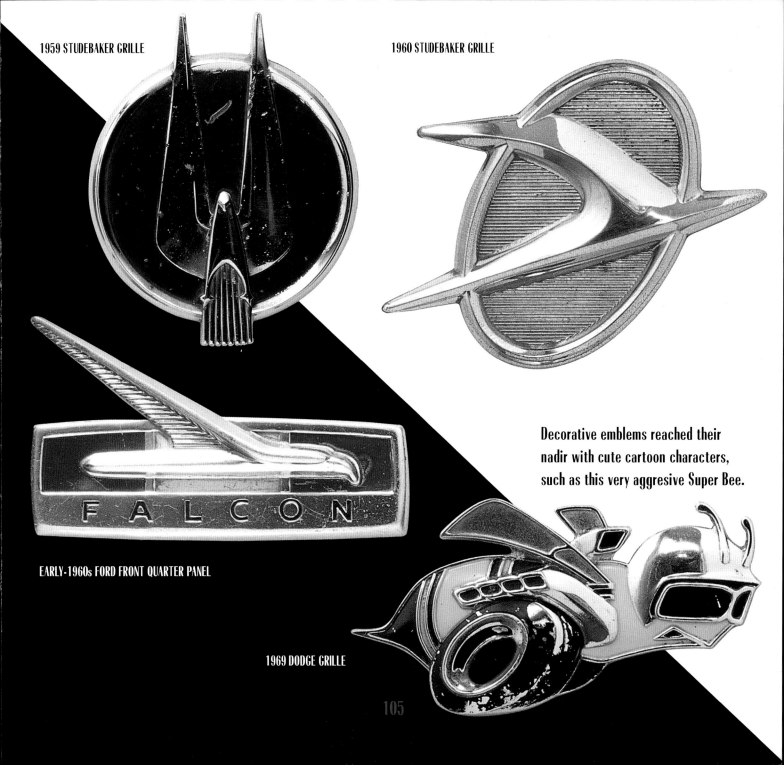

1959 STUDEBAKER GRILLE

1960 STUDEBAKER GRILLE

EARLY-1960s FORD FRONT QUARTER PANEL

FALCON

Decorative emblems reached their nadir with cute cartoon characters, such as this very aggresive Super Bee.

1969 DODGE GRILLE

105

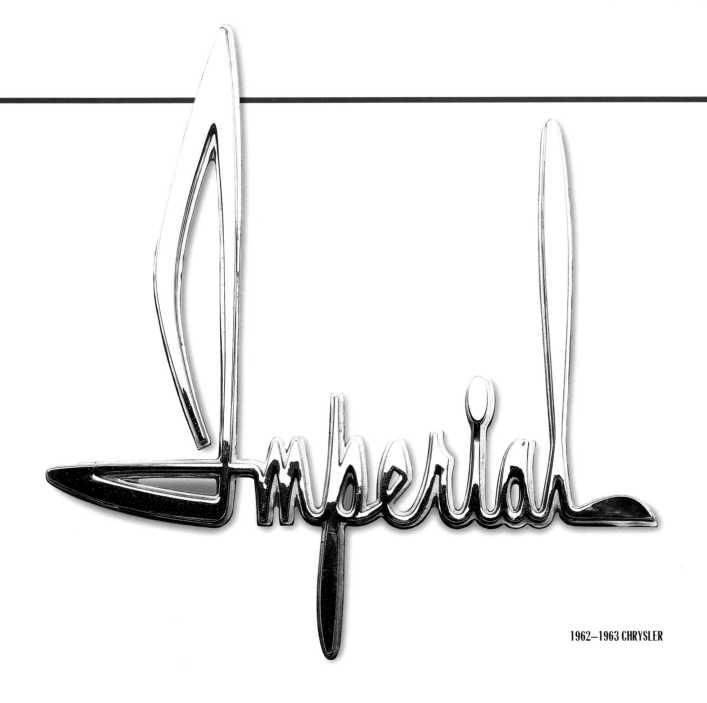

1962–1963 CHRYSLER

SCRIPT

Automotive script incorporates both form and content. Those collectors interested in the aesthetics of typography and calligraphy will find an abundance of styles and fonts. Because it made sense to fabricate these pieces as a single unit, freehand faces abounded. If type was used it was generally unified by a design element of some sort, usually a strike-through or underline. While prewar script tended towards art deco motifs, postwar script had a distinct "anything goes!" sensibility.

Content included many weird and wonderful expressions that only advertising copywriters could produce. We had Ultramatic, Futuramic, Dynaflow, and Super Deluxe. All are essentially meaningless, but they were "Concepts As Modern As Tomorrow, At Your Dealer Today!" Little has changed. Today's autos give us Cab-forward, Positraction, and Onstar—whatever that means!

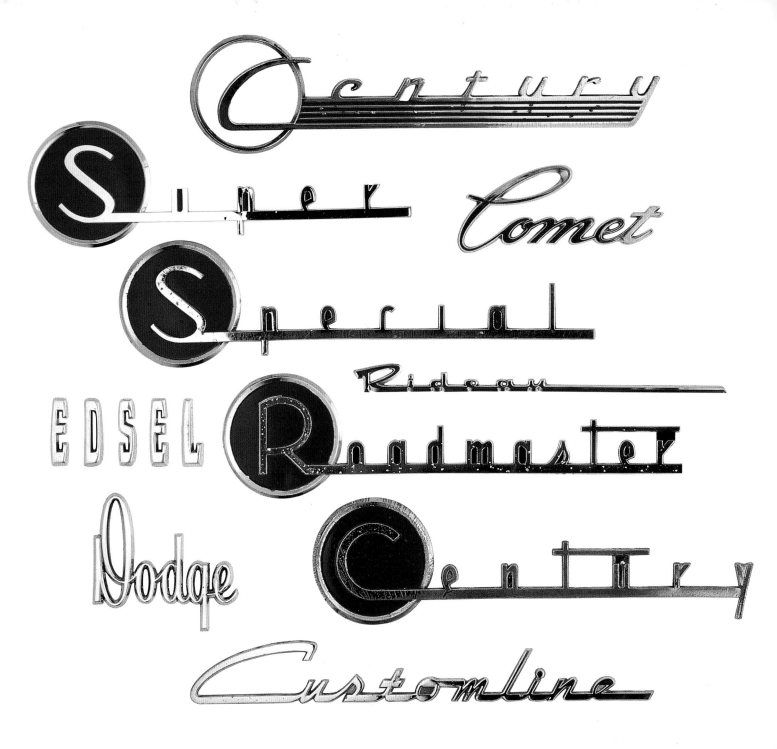

Star Chief

Fireflite

Mayfair

Meteor

FIREDOME

Cadillac

Packard

 *Sabre*

LeSabre

LeSabre

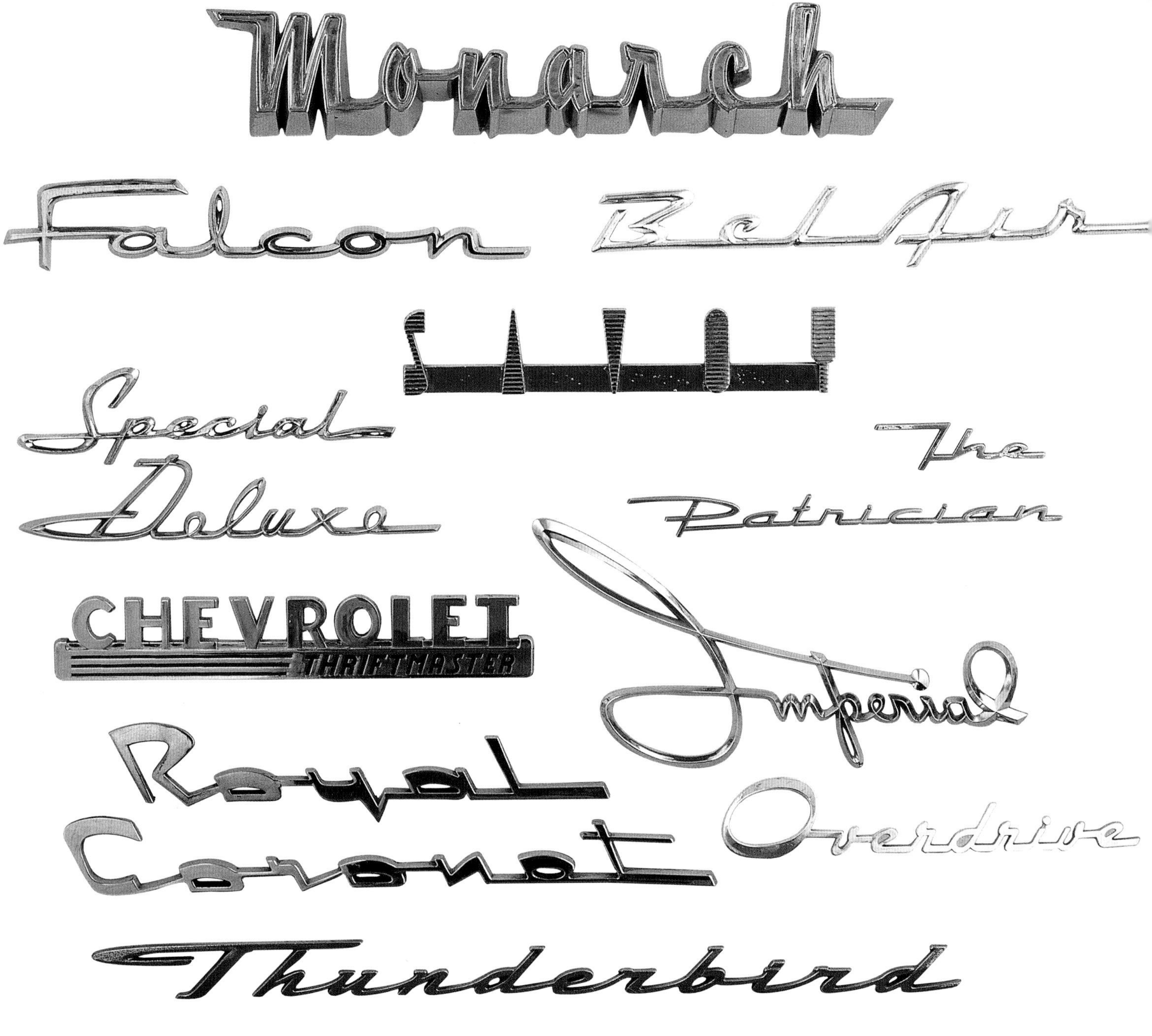

Monarch

Falcon

Bel Air

Special
Deluxe

The
Patrician

CHEVROLET
THRIFTMASTER

Imperial

Royal
Coronet

Overdrive

Thunderbird

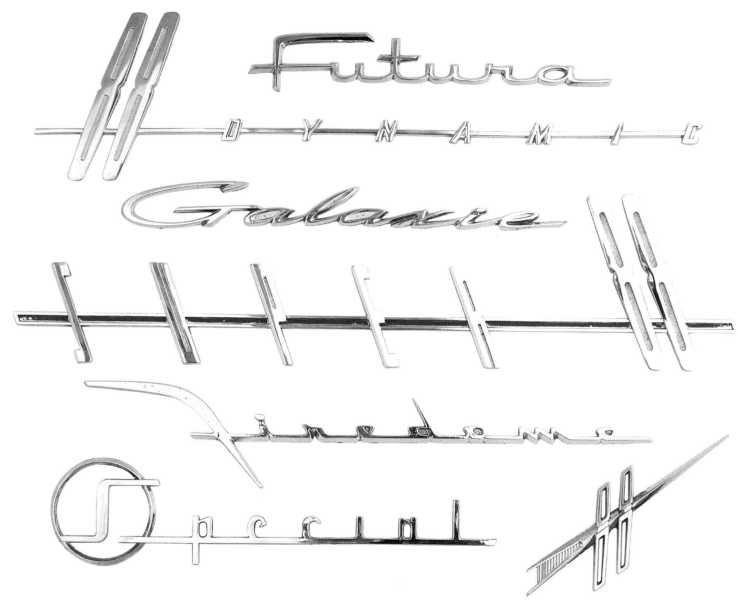

Falcon

SUPER
DELUXE

Super

Futura

Plymouth

MERCURY Comet

Overdrive Custom

F 85

Richelieu

Dodge Lancer

Ultramatic